GRATITUDE TO GREATNESS

Proven Practices Producing Profound Success

BURHAN UDDIN

Praise for

GRATITUDE TO GREATNESS

Proven Practices Producing Profound Success

'…when you have free time do read brother Burhan's book, it's a good read… and it's quite good for people who are looking for motivation and some discipline.'

- **Sheikh Abu Ubayd**, Founder & CEO of Dar Al-Arqam, Dean of Studies at Dar Al-Arqam, Speaker and Consultant

'I immediately connected to the content of this book. It taught me that our mindsets need to be in line with our heart and it gave me those mindsets to become a much better person.'

- **Asim, M**, Co-Founder and Host of Ibn Battuta's Boat, Marketing analyst

'The book was very beneficial and took steps towards faith and philosophy without specifically contaminating itself to any one particular belief. Very motivational for those seeking peace.'

- **Sahim C**, Serial Entrepreneur and Consultant

'It was really an eye opener. Before reading the book, I didn't see the bigger picture of gratitude and all the things covered in the book. Didn't expect it to have a massive impact on the day to day life. After reading the book, it helped me to have a different perspective and better view of life. I enjoyed the deeper meaning and detailed context of the book.'

- **Musleh, U**, Entrepreneur and Flagship Store Manager

Gratitude to Greatness © *2019 Burhan Uddin*

Get your FREE 2 Key Mindsets to Unlock Your Utmost Potential PDF: bit.ly/twokeymindsets

Disclaimer

This book has been written to provide motivation and information to our readers. It is sold with the understanding that the author is not engaged to render any type of psychological, legal, or any other kind of professional advice. The instructions and advice in this book are not intended as a substitute for counselling. The content within this book is the sole expression and opinion of its author. Any perceived slight of individuals or organisations is completely unintentional. No warranties or guarantees are expressed or implied by the author's choice to include any of the content in this book. The author shall not be liable for any physical, psychological, emotional, financial or commercial damages, including but not limited to, special, incidental, consequential or other damages. Our views and rights are the same:

-You must test everything for yourself according to your own situations, talents and aspirations.

-You are responsible for your own decisions, choice, actions and results.

Get your FREE Gratitude Process Sheet PDF:

bit.ly/gratitudeprocesssheet

TABLE OF CONTENTS

* * * * *

Introduction

We all reach points in our lives where despite us continuing to seek the 'good' feeling that we subconsciously yearn for, this good feeling just doesn't enter our hearts. It's because we have been focusing too much on what we *want* to achieve and hardly any time on what we already have.

Human beings as part of their natural disposition, need to be grateful for the goodness they have been given. However, it is a choice they have to make consciously.

Many would not regularly express gratitude for their blessings. The feelings of laziness, discomfort of exercising the brain and ignorance of the long term beneficial effects of doing so, are factors behind this reality.

Gratitude is a generous gift that is placed on the table for all of us. We just need to acknowledge that gift, take it and use it.

A world without gratitude is sad, dull, depressive, purposeless and can even lead to suicide. We hear many stories of those who when they had lost large amounts of money, their partner whom they deeply loved left them or a similar calamity that had befallen them, lead them to suicide. Why? They did not practice gratitude daily for the basic things they have, especially on aspects such as being content with the worst cases scenarios, realising that their state would still be a *dream* life for people in most parts of the world. If they do so, they would be the furthest away from suicide. Look at how vital it is for us to exercise daily gratitude. That it keeps us far away from even losing our life by our own hands!

Consistently being grateful will change our lives to one where our heart and soul subconsciously feels and says 'that feels deeply natural, that's what I've been searching for, that is how I'm supposed to be feeling.' Feelings of deep tranquillity, fulfillment, satisfaction, happiness, serenity and peace fill our hearts.

Gratitude is an innate value we should maintain and enhance so that it shoots us through the obstacles of life to eventually achieve our lofty ambitions and goals. In other words, get through life easily.

As a matter of fact, it is known amongst those who are striving towards achieving a lofty goal, whether it is to become a billionaire, an owner of the next big online e-commerce platform or changing civilisation for the better, that a portion of their time ought to be spent in gratitude. This would rejuvenate them, thereby bring a natural healthy motivation which arises from realising the great achievements, success and blessings they already have.

Gratitude has been a major part of my life and it is a big factor behind the achievements I have attained in the last decade. I've had a low point in my life a decade ago. Ever since then, I was guided and inspired to research for solutions, coming to realise some important grand principles which have succoured me. One of those was gratitude which included 'being content with the worst case scenario.' Looking back now, I'm ever so grateful for going through that low point in my life as it is a blessing in disguise and has lead me to experiencing the great quality of life I am living in right now. My life has been an amazing journey since that low point and I am privileged with this opportunity to share some of the great points of benefit I have accumulated. And I hope you will gain deep value for what I'm about to share. That is my aim.

This book has been written concisely so that it is not a long read, especially if your life is very busy. So that you don't give yourself excuses of not having time to read it.

I hope you can benefit comprehensively on this topic of gratitude and know exactly how to practically enact it in your life.

The content in this book are the fruits of my decades worth of study, research, grasping of facts and realities, experience and reflection. Thereby, unique content has been presented here that I hope will completely transform your life and perception to one that is rich in positivity which drives you to grandeur success.

In this book, you will understand gratitude from a wide range of angles. I will provide practical measures for you to embark on the journey of enacting gratitude so that you experience the deep tranquillity and joy of life that results from this embarkment. Looking at it from another perspective, this book will give you enlightenment, insight, inspiration and motivation that transforms you to becoming a person of grand personality, shining with the trait of gratitude.

I hope this book impacts your heart in a deeply effective manner whereby your life is changed completely to one with a higher level of well-being, prosperity and happiness.

I will now begin this innate yearning journey into the world of the hearts and minds magnifying the characteristic of gratitude.

CHAPTER 1
Definition of Gratitude

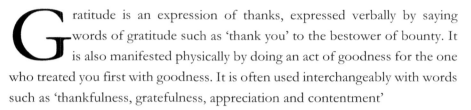

Gratitude is an expression of thanks, expressed verbally by saying words of gratitude such as 'thank you' to the bestower of bounty. It is also manifested physically by doing an act of goodness for the one who treated you first with goodness. It is often used interchangeably with words such as 'thankfulness, gratefulness, appreciation and contentment'

Gratitude is a powerful inner trait that is recognised universally. Human beings all over the world recognise this universal innate value and would by sheer nature, give more value to one who embodies this trait.

It brings an increase in return of bounties. Many of us can testify to this reality through the array of experiences we have had.

"Practice gratitude consistently and experience a wave of light filled with tranquillity, contentment, satisfaction, serenity, peace, fulfillment happiness, bliss and joy fill your world."

CHAPTER 2
WHY Should I Be Grateful?

The *why* for any of our goals is at the heart of success in the long run. Books have been written *only* on the importance of knowing our *whys*. Therefore, I will now bring to light some of the important *whys* pertaining to having gratitude.

2.1 Easily 'grind': the heart of progression

Exercising gratitude will help us easily grind during the day. What will make it easy is being in a state and feeling of tranquillity, satisfaction, fulfillment, contentment, peace, serenity, joy and happiness as opposed to stressed, frustrated, annoyed and angry. These negative feelings are a recompense for focusing in the long term only on what we desire to achieve and not on that which we already have achieved. In other words, these negative feelings have surfaced as a repercussion for not being a person of gratitude by routinely spending time everyday expressing thanks for the gifts/successes we have been given already.

Routinely expressing gratitude makes it easier to do what is right despite not feeling to. By not expressing gratitude daily, we can feel low, in turn, do that which isn't in line with our priorities. This brings feelings of weakness and guilt into our hearts. Examples of this include doing too much of one type of work because you enjoy it at the expense of another when you know that by prioritising the latter, you'll progress faster towards your goal. We do that which we enjoy and not the priority because we don't feel good. In other words, we need the good feelings that gratitude brings to easily be consistent in doing that which is line with our priorities, thereby progress towards our goals exponentially faster.

Grinding is at 'the heart of progression' because it is at the core of achieving any lofty aims. Why is it core? **It is core, since** without grinding, especially when we don't feel like taking action, we won't practically progress towards our goals. Without grinding, we absolutely cannot succeed at anything hence why it is at the heart of progression'.

2.2 Gratitude rescues rough relationships before its collapse

When gratitude enters our relationships, meaning we remember the goodness done to us by our spouse let's say and thank them for it, our relationship will be filled with tranquillity, love, kindness, compassion, peace, joy, satisfaction, serenity, happiness, fulfillment and more. Expressing thanks here includes verbally uttering words of thankfulness for the good they have done to us or performing an action of appreciation such as buying a gift, leaving a love note or treating the person to something they love.

I remember reading about the works of a marriage councillor who would hold seminars, training people on the art of gratitude in marriage and cultivating the principle of gratitude for those who are on the verge of divorce in their marriages. They would coach their clients how by applying this simple, yet grand law of success, they can fix their relationship up completely. And that is what happened. In the end, they thanked the councillor for providing a great noble service to them. I was amazed to see how gratitude takes them from zero to hero, so to speak.

If gratitude fixes the most complex relationship an individual usually undergoes in their life, then application of it in all our other relationships will by far, generate a deep positive impact, thus bring to us a life filled with an abundance of well-being, satisfaction, happiness, contentment, harmony, peace etc.

Looking at it from a different perspective, through employing gratitude, the stress, frustration, pain and hurt caused by your loved ones when you didn't act in accordance with their expectation, diminishes. And therefore, subconsciously, you would feel delight and your heart will feel spacious instead of constriction. As a result, freedom and happiness will emanate since you've freed yourself from the negative feelings and have only positive ones. And therefore, you can progress towards your goal multiple times faster without diminishing in quality What a great investment gratitude is!

> *"When we've reached our lowest point in life where we find it deathly difficult to continue, gratitude it is, that takes us from zero to hero."*

CHAPTER 3

Deep Destructions Emerging From Ungratefulness

3.1 Selfishness (or greed)

When we are not being grateful, whether that be by not recalling our blessings routinely or thanking someone for their favour, we can fall into being full of ourselves. In other words, self-centred. All we think about is how to benefit ourselves. And therefore, we become selfish. The love for personal success blinds us from the reality that we cannot achieve great goals except by collaborating with other people. And in order to successfully work with other people we cannot just think about ourselves. Otherwise people will find it difficult to collaborate with us because they are harmed by our selfish attitude. How can they be harmed? Their needs can be unmet because of the uncaring attitude the other person displays. They can feel low, weak, degraded and devalued when around them, which slows down or halts their development.

On the contrary, by being grateful, we come to realise we have attained success already and additional success that we achieve is a bonus. Therefore, I can spare some time to grant my attention to those in need of it. I can spare some time to help out a loved one with something they cannot solve easily. As a matter of fact, by giving value to others, we will actually be moving at a vaster pace towards our goal. And there are a number of ways this process takes place. Here are two ways:

1. Receiving relevant guidelines on achieving our goal: giving value to others through gratitude brings up a warm conversation of good will. You will express what's in your heart and mind - matters on achieving your lofty goal let's say - to the one whom you have expressed gratitude to (usually a family member, relative or friend). You have expressed appreciation so they would naturally feel to do good in return. They could provide some mindsets, angles of perception and beneficial advice that didn't even cross your mind! One sentence from these

mindsets, angles of perception and beneficial advice alone can actually change the entire game plan for your goal to a whole new level! That's why the concept of 'mastermind' originated from Napolean Hill in his book The Law of Success, is recognised amongst entrepreneurs, millionaires and billionaires because of exactly this procedure. Someone in the mastermind group shares a vital piece of knowledge relevant to you that changes your game plan completely to a whole new level. This makes you become a billionaire let's say. So suppose you regularly receive advice and insight in return for expressing appreciation to someone. You will achieve your goal at a tremendously faster pace compared to before.

2. Law of reciprocal: in other words, 'what goes around comes around'. This is similar to the first process. When you benefit someone, the law of reciprocal dictates that they will want to benefit you back. Usually, when we help someone at the time of 'need,' we would hear words similar to the following: 'if ever you need anything, let me know. It's the least I can do.' If you had a conversation with them and they came to know of your situation and what you're trying to achieve, they could recommend someone who is an expert in the field you're in. Or they themselves may be experienced in that regards and could help you progress a lot faster towards your goal. Again, like I stated in point number 1 above, this piece of advice can change your game plan around 360 degrees pushing you forward with a new approach, that is multiple times more efficient. Again, the pace at which you progress towards your goal will be vaster than before.

Sometimes, the *difference* in the speed of progression prior to the advice being given and after the advice has been given, is *phenomenal*. You move at ten or more times the speed towards your goal than before you manifested the advice.

Wisdom can lie with anyone. Hence why it is important that we realise what value gratitude can bring through the law of reciprocal and take advantage of this 'profitable investment that will always give you returns'.

3.2 Selfishness breeds harsh heartedness which brings your goal to a collapse

When we don't exercise gratitude regularly after falling into selfishness, if this state lasts for a long time without being fixed, it is somewhat dangerous. How? Our moral fibre becomes weak which means the humanness we feel begins to disappear. We feel animalistic. As if we're in a jungle and it is about survival of the fittest. This gets reflected in our attitude towards people. Since we don't value them, we start communicating to them without making them feel valued. In other words, lacking respect for them. We can sound somewhat blunt or rude in our tone. That is because subconsciously we perceive them to be like ourself - selfish. In that state, we think people just care about themselves. If the people in society were to be selfish like this, in the long run, society will crumble. The strength of the society will disintegrate.

A society that is not selfish but rather caring and helpful, is like ropes tied to each other in a circle very tightly. If people grab it with both their fists on either end of the circle and try to rip it apart, it would be difficult to do so. Seeing as it is tied strongly, if those ropes were to not be tied at all, we can obviously see that it is already apart. No one even has to come to try and break the bond between them. They're already broken. In other words, the society is broken. Thus, weakness is triggered in the economy. One of these ropes that are apart from each other represent someone who is selfish and harsh hearted. All the ropes represent people who are selfish and harsh hearted in society. We can see how on a deeper level, societal and economical dangers prompt from not adopting gratitude in our lives. This is because the exclusion of this trait leads to selfishness, harsh heartedness, in turn, crumbling of the society resulting in people having a lower quality of life. They also lose privileges they once had prior to the appearance of this subtle virus known as moral degeneration.

Moreover, the lofty goal you sought to achieve can collapse into failure owing to the fact that harsh heartedness makes people flee from you. They don't trust you because there is a foul stench emanating from you which they can't bear to be around, so to speak. The foul stench is the selfishness and harsh heartedness. If one has arrived at this station of state but then woke up to the reality and learnt their lesson to not be selfish, it's of course better than one who is in the same state without learning their lesson. However, the long spell of time spent being in that state has wasted a lot of time and caused damage to: their reputation, trust and reliability. They would now have to work really hard to return to their best state again.

To conclude, we can see how embodiment of gratitude is wisdom. It is the mother of vast goodness and preventer of chaos in society.

3.3 Rushing

A by-product that can ensue when leaving out gratitude from our lives is *rushing*. When we narrow our focus to our wants only, we can get caught up in doing things fast, being on autopilot. In other words, we act without thinking. What tends to be the outcome when we go about our lives like this, is losing productivity and efficiency. How? Well, if I am on autopilot, I would not really be thinking and asking myself from time to time important questions such as 'is this the best way to continue on at the current stage? Am I prioritising in the best way? Am I doing everything I'm supposed to so that the product/service delivered is of utmost quality?' Through acknowledging the answers to these questions and applying them, we can be more efficient and productive. Rushing diminishes this productivity and efficiency.

By continuing to rush, we can actually make mistakes and waste time because automation in our action denotes deficiency in consciousness-we're just following our feelings without really thinking. And we all know that giving precedence to feelings over the intellect entails corruption. In addition, we know that the one who rushes, is bound to make many mistakes because he isn't thinking clearly before deciding to do an action. On the other hand, by being grateful, we become humbled and sincere. This leads to wanting to do that which is correct and best. Of the things which are correct and best are doing things at a moderate pace. Gratitude will propel us to do things at a moderate pace because after expressing it, we would feel successful already. We therefore would find it easier to discipline ourself by not allowing ourself to rush as we would realise that rushing, despite appearing outwardly as if it is helping us move faster towards our goal - a move that is unwise - will actually slow us down in the long run. And because we would make many mistakes and bear the harms emanating from them, we would feel demotivated and think it is really hard to succeed in this type of business project, venture etc. Not realising the reality, that our approach of being hasty has lead us to feeling like this.

Rushing leads to the disappearance of sincerity. After rushing for some time, we will feel dullness in our hearts because rushing makes us lose focus on the purpose for which we are working towards our goal. And eventually this leads to feeling demotivated and lazy, which can make us feel weak, not good, stressed, frustrated, annoyed, thereby making us resort to going beyond our limits. This makes us lose discipline and at times can be dangerous as we can fall from a mountain and break into pieces, so to speak. In other words, we can fall back on our achievements. If one is in this state, it will take some time before they can return back to their best. And just to add a point of benefit, the degree to which we exert our efforts to return back to our best state will be higher compared to the degree to which we would have had to exert (that will progress us to a better state even), if we did what we were supposed to do in the first place. And that is of not going beyond our limits when we felt inclined towards doing so. Going beyond our limits include spending more time on: social media, hanging out with friends, playing games, sleeping, eating etc. Furthermore, we have lost out much potential progression towards our goal, seeing as the rate of progression is exponential over time. To make matters more clear, if we go back on our achievements due to one slip up, we can end up losing months of progression. In addition, if we want to be a champion in what we do, we cannot afford to slip up because our competitors will probably be exhausting all their efforts, so we need to do even better than them. Going back to the main point, we can see from the points above, the deep devastating effects of not making gratitude a daily habit.

To conclude, all of the deep destructions you have read above are eye opening reasons for us to adopt the habit of gratitude which, as you have seen so far, prevents many harmful behaviours and attitudes from appearing as a result, that can lead to utter destruction, losing out on achieving the goal we desired. Beyond the reasons I have mentioned already for why we should express regular gratitude, there are many more. You need to ask yourself and discover why you are being grateful as you will have a specific scenario with a specific *why* that motivates you effectively.

"Gratitude glides you to your great goal of glory."

CHAPTER 4
Enhancing Our Level of Gratitude

O ver time, through regular expression of gratitude, we may aspire to be grateful at a higher level. So here are two ways to enhance this magnificent trait within us:

4.1 The Golden Mindset – 'Do what is right and best whether you like it or not'

By applying what I have written in the subheading above, we will truly be exercising gratitude. In other words, being content with choosing the option we think is best at the current moment even though we feel like choosing the other option because it is more fun, enjoyable, easy or has reasons similar to that nature.

Sometimes, out of our passion, we want to do something which is not necessarily harmful but we know during that moment we should prioritise another task that is more important. For example, whilst embarking on my journey doing entrepreneurial research, there have been times where I was supposed to give attention to my family. I can sense from my intuition that my family members seem to feel as if I don't care about them. My passion for progressing is something I have to battle with at this stage. So I would think and see the sequential effects of choosing to focus on my entrepreneurial work instead of prioritising a short amount of time, maybe 30 minutes maximum, for my family. Rather, I've come to realise the *golden mindset*: 'do what is right and best whether you like it or not'. It is golden because doing what is right and best leads us to attaining our goals exponentially faster than otherwise.

Spending time socialising with my family members has propelled me faster towards my goal giving me the following benefits: taking a break from the day's grind; feel a positive atmosphere (that arose after making my family members feel loved and cared for) at home wherein I was able to feel energetic, in turn, more productive. If I didn't give any attention to my family member(s) that day because of my passion and finding of enjoyment in conducting entrepreneurial research, then that would be selfishness. Self-centredness would creep in. This would incur negativity as selfishness breeds many harms, some of which I have mentioned in chapter 3. As a result, I would not be able to concentrate on tasks that would progress me towards my goal. Also, not doing what is right will play on my mind subconsciously, in turn, I would not be productive and efficient. Hence why it is of utmost importance that we realise the depth of the *golden mindset* I have mentioned in this paragraph-a simple principle yet the most grandeur in value. Let's also realise that application of this concept is a sign of gratitude/contentment since we are willing to sacrifice in the short run to do the right and best thing. And usually those who deep down are content with the worst case scenario, would sacrifice to do what is right and best.

To reiterate the power of this *golden mindset,* let's look at the cause and effect of providing our family members with what they need, in this case 'attention': by spending a short amount of time to give attention, show care and love – the causes - I would actually progress further in the long term – the effect. It is a universal law which I and many of us have experienced in effect many times - that when we help others, we receive help back. 'What goes around comes around' as they say. The help and positivity we receive back are amongst the effects which help us to progress more in the long run. And just to add, knowing very well from experience that 'if I decide to not oppose myself to do that which I know is more important at that point of time I would end up achieving less' helps to enact the *golden mindset.* Amongst the negative effects of giving more care to my personal wants than what others need is feeling lonely, weak and heartless. These are the outcome of being selfish.

To conclude, the more consistent we are on the *golden mindset,* the higher our level of gratitude and contentment, thus the faster the level of progression towards our goal/dream.

4.2 Sacrifice and help people

When we go out of our way to look for opportunities to sacrifice and help people, whether it is by giving some money or buying food for the needy, helping an old lady cross the road or carrying her shopping bags for her etc., it humbles us, making us feel grateful, happy and satisfied inside. It makes us feel grateful because by seeing their needy situation we feel grateful that we haven't been placed in that situation. As soon as we genuinely realise that and it registers in our heart, we begin to feel that tranquillity and peace entering it. If we regularly adopt this mindset in addition to our daily expression of gratitude, we surely would reach higher levels of gratitude which means *deeper* feelings of tranquillity, happiness, peace, serenity, satisfaction, fulfillment and joy.

"If only you knew the humongous harms dispelled as a gift for being grateful..."

CHAPTER 5
Practical Application

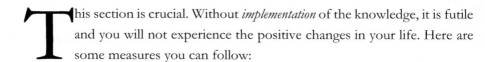

This section is crucial. Without *implementation* of the knowledge, it is futile and you will not experience the positive changes in your life. Here are some measures you can follow:

5.1 Spend 10-15 minutes everyday expressing gratitude

In the morning, spend 10-15 minutes expressing thanks for what you have, by first asking yourself questions such as: 'What have I been blessed with? What have I already achieved? What do I have that others don't? Etc. And thereafter *genuinely think* to find the answers to these questions and acknowledge the great bounties you have. I personally adopt this practice whilst having breakfast as doing so means I hit 2 birds with 1 stone. In other words, I complete the task of having breakfast and expressing gratitude at the same time. Therefore, I have 10-15 minutes extra compared to someone who spends 10-15 minutes after breakfast for expressing gratitude.

Now, of course, you don't have to follow it exactly as I set it out here. You can decide to spend 10-15 minutes first thing in the morning. The morning would be a good time since expressing gratitude at this time is one chosen by entrepreneurs to help them grind it out for the day. Also, expressing gratitude at the beginning of the day means you start your day positively which helps you easily get through the challenges and obstacles of the day. I personally have experienced how deeply effective it has been for me.

5.2 Recalling our lowest point in life that has changed us completely for the better - a deep and powerful gratitude technique

There is one technique that has been extremely effective in motivating me back to continuing on when life's challenges felt so rigid that I felt like giving up. Those of us who have experienced a very low point in life followed by successfully overcoming it actually possess an extremely powerful tool. By recalling this point of feeling the lowness you have felt and how you overcame it, such as discerning you have nothing to lose, you will come to know that you have achieved so much since that low point in your life. Soon after recalling this, you would feel a deep level of gratitude, in turn, tranquillity, happiness, peace etc.

In addition, if you were willing to continue on towards your goal with the mindset of 'I have nothing to lose so I will try again' you will powerfully cut through any difficult challenges that obstruct your way. What this mindset means is that if I fail, I will get up and try again. And usually, prior to recalling this mindset, fear of failure surfaces. Through this mindset, you will not fear failure and overcome any tendencies for perfectionism.

I need to stress the importance of actually taking the time to recall that scenario of our lowest point in life as accurately as possible. This is so that we can: truly feel how it felt; realise what helped us to overcome it; remember how humbled we felt; remember how we were willing to be content with whatever we achieve thereafter, especially if that experience of low feeling was one that included being on the brink of death; realise and truly feel how close we were to death and that if death took over us we would not be able to achieve anything we wanted to-so since that point until now, whatever we have achieved is a bonus because if we had died, we of course cannot achieve anything thereafter. By thinking and feeling in these ways, we would reap its fruits by experiencing a flood of tranquillity, peace, happiness and contentment filling our hearts. And that would propel us to pace faster towards our lofty pursuits.

5.3 Grand Realisations

For a lot of us, there are some common grand favours we can always recall that will bring us deep positive feelings gratitude brings, so long as we truly acknowledge and feel their value in our hearts. These are the following:

1. Functions of the body: eyes, ears, mouth, nose, hands, feet etc. There are people out there who are deaf, dumb, blind or paralysed. If we were like them, we can hardly do anything, let alone achieve our goals. Rather, we would have

to rely on someone who is compassionate, caring and merciful to look after us. If they didn't take care of us, we would suffer: we cannot take pleasure in observing the beautiful sceneries that exist upon on the Earth; we cannot have a good time socialising with others; we cannot move around the world freely; we cannot enjoy the adventure, thrill and satisfaction of working towards achieving our goals and many more.

a) Here is an exercise you can do to actualise the elegant beauty and magnificent power your eyes hold: close your eyes for 10 seconds. Continue to keep your eyes closed after those 10 seconds. Imagine you actually couldn't see anymore and had to live like that. Try to walk around whilst your eyes are closed. See if you can do something as simple as getting yourself a glass of water, watch a video or read the newspaper. No doubt, it would be very difficult or impossible. Imagine you had to continue the rest of your life like this. How hard would your life now be? Slowly, begin to open your eyes. Acknowledge that which you can see with those very pair of eyes. You'll feel taken aback at the sheer magnificence and beauty of your vision - the clarity and detail with which we can see things. How easy is it for us to watch an important video? We don't need to pay money for our eyes to open up so that we can watch something. Rather, we have the power to open this tool effortlessly, to benefit from it for free as many times as we wish. It is an enormous blessing we must realise. With it we can benefit from countless services. People will pay millions to be able to see if they were blind. So in that sense, we are actually millionaires. And that is because if people are willing to pay millions for functions of their body that are disabled to get it working whilst our functions are working, we are actually possessors of tools worth millions. We can attain vast benefits, enjoyments and services through them, hence their worth.

b) Now, you will learn about an ear exercise you can do to relish the natural vibrant sounds you hear. Try blocking your ears by pushing the small outer section next to the hole of the ear inwards using your fingers. Again, like we did for the eyes, keep it in that position for 10 seconds. Slowly release your fingers and acknowledge, similar to what you did for the eyes, the natural beauty and elegance of the sounds around you. It feels fresh and refreshing. Those who have experienced blocked ears and underwent the use of syringe to unblock their ears will usually appreciate them more than those who haven't.

2. Independency and basic necessities of life: we have been saved from dependency. Suppose you are disabled or paralysed and the one whom you are dependent upon, such as your parent, sibling or an assigned carer, is not financially stable. You will live a life of struggle and have no choice out of it. What is worse than that, is being disabled and not having any dependents to look after you. Your life would be more of a struggle since you don't know how to take care of your needs in the most easiest and efficient of ways. Thus, you would take the harder route to fulfil your basic needs. That is the life of an orphan who has no one to look after him and has not been left any wealth by his parents. Imagine living the life of such an orphan. Not knowing how to speak, not having any clothes to wear, just helpless really because you don't know how to do anything. We are so blessed to be living in satisfactory accommodation; sleeping comfortably in beds; eating healthy, delicious food; drinking clean water everyday without having to leave our homes; receiving a good education; given opportunities to do noble works for the society; enjoy learning and developing; enjoy socialising; going out to eat at restaurants, trying a variety of succulent dishes and not facing any challenges of survival. We are indeed living a dream life compared to *most* people of the world. This is something known and also proven by statistics. Let's realise that had we been an individual living on the other side of the globe such as the African region, which is struggling to find enough water and food just to live every single day, we would also dream to be living a life of someone in a developed country. We would be dreaming to live the life of one who is almost guaranteed fresh, clean water and food everyday. So let's cherish the high quality of life we are living in and be immensely grateful for having more than enough food and water to function on everyday.

3. Quality education and opportunities: realise there are millions of people across the world who aren't getting any education let alone education to a high standard. They don't have the best of opportunities and facilities like we do here in the developed countries. They dream to one day be a pilot, doctor, engineer,

judge etc., but it looks impossible for them to actualise. On the contrary, we have all the resources needed right before us, to easily succeed in becoming something we've always dreamt of. But because we don't realise the value of what we have, we become lazy, in turn, find it difficult to study or be committed and devoted to achieve that which we yearn for.

There are some countries that provide education but they don't have the best of resources or facilities with which to study and complete their research. Examples of this include countries from the Asian subcontinent.

I know of an individual who has come to the UK from an Asian developing country telling me how easy it is to pass exams and attain degrees here because they find quick access to all the facilities and resources to study and complete their assignment. When they were in their home country, they would strive extremely hard to study and complete their assignments despite the lack of resources and facilities. Later on, when they came to the UK, they saw how they don't have to exert painstaking effort to complete their studies and succeed in their assignments. They now feel appreciative and grateful for what they have, therefore take full advantage of the resources and facilities, coming out with exceptional grades. Then, due to their gratitude mindset which motivates them to take full advantage of the resources at their disposal, working really hard simultaneously, they end up attaining their dreams easily. Some of them cannot even speak the English language properly yet they achieve better than those who can and have been brought up in the UK since birth.

So how can those of us living in developed countries realise the value of the facilities, resources and opportunities we have to achieve our dreams? Here are two powerful ways:

1. Reflection: we take some time out to reflect and realise how fortunate we are compared to the millions of other people without education and opportunities like us. And that those in other parts of the globe have resources and facilities, the standard of which is very low compared to us. In other words, we have the best of everything compared to the rest of the world.

2. Watch videos, documentaries, read books and articles pertaining to the lifestyle of those without education and opportunities in developing countries: this can help us practically actualise how it must be for them. When we see it with our own eyes and understand how they're feeling, it will be more impactful, thus we will appreciate the great blessings of education and opportunities we have.

5.4 Witness people who are struggling and living lives of a lower standard

To see something in real life is highly impactful. Therefore, if we see the miserable, weak, poor, hard and painful conditions others are in, we would truly be appreciative of the standard of life we have been gifted with. Here are some practical impactful actions we can take to achieve this:

- Visit hospitals to witness patients. When we visit the hospital, we will find patients undergoing various struggles and pains. We find patients suffering with tumour, cancer or in a state severely wounded from accidents (such as car collisions). Others would be in a coma, have lost their memory etc. By comparing their lives to ours, we can realise how abundantly fortunate we are. Those patients would be willing to pay anything to be in the good healthy state we are in.

- Speak to beggars to visualise and realise the hardship, discomfort and struggles they have to undertake on a daily basis. By comparing this to our own life and acknowledging how we don't have to go through any of that, we would indeed feel immensely grateful.

- Travel to poor countries to witness their daily life. Witnessing how they would travel for miles just to collect a bucket load of water and the hard work they exert daily to find food. If we compare their life to ours, we would realise how easy our lives are since our basic needs of food, water and shelter are met without any painstaking effort.

By engaging in the above activities with a genuine intention of learning and feeling the struggles and hardships other people are facing as well as comparing their lives to ours, we surely would be deeply impacted with positivity. It will make us emotional, in turn, humble us. We would realise how fortunate we are to have been blessed with a good standard of life because the quality of life people have been given since they came into this world is not something they chose. Hence, it would motivate us to be kind to the poor and help them, thus make us better human beings. And it will instill within our hearts, deep feelings of tranquillity, serenity, peace, happiness, satisfaction, fufillment, joy and contentment through which we can achieve our goals faster, living an amazing life.

CHAPTER 6

Practical Stages for an Easier Routine of Gratitude

————⫸•⫷————

To achieve anything in life, we have to go through stages. It is a universal law that must be actualised. In this chapter, I will highlight some stages that are vital in the long term to develop and enhance the characteristic of gratitude within us.

Stage 1- Realising and remembering *why* we should be grateful

The *why* is a major factor behind all lofty successes and legacies. Many successful people will prioritise teaching us the deep power of knowing our *whys*. So what you should first do is simply reflect on the *reasons* for wanting to be a person of gratitude. Here are two important and common reasons people have:

1. Realising that gratitude will improve the quality of your life in all spheres. This includes relationships, work, business and personal goals. It will rejuvenate your motivation for the task at hand, thus enjoy the process of accomplishing something. This motivation is due to the feelings of tranquillity, contentment, joy, happiness, serenity, satisfaction, fulfillment and peace you feel from realising how successful and blessed you already are. As a result, you are able to grind easily, which means you will achieve exponentially more in the long term compared to the case where you didn't exercise gratitude in the first place – due to not remembering why you should be grateful. In other words, you will achieve your goal faster than others who don't exercise regular gratitude as a result of not regularly remembering why they should enact gratitude.

2. Realising that if you aren't expressing gratitude regularly, harmful consequences can result. These include being greedy, miserly, full of yourself, sad, lonely and weak. This can all lead you to end up not succeeding in your aspirations. So you may want to weigh up the pros and cons and say to yourself: 'if being ungrateful can lead me to losing my job, being unsuccessful with business and life, then *I have to be grateful as a duty, whether I like it or not.*' Of course

the reality is people enjoy exercising gratitude and feeling its positive feelings but having the mindset of '...*whether I like it or not*' brings forth a strong willpower which helps you to be consistent in regularly expressing gratitude. So here and there when you don't feel like expressing gratitude, you continue doing so regardless. This mindset will inculcate in you a deep want for yourself to do whatever it takes to achieve your endeavours.

Just to add, realise that some reasons will be more effective for you specifically than others. Over time, after regularly asking yourself *why* you want to have gratitude in your life and genuinely thinking with your heart and mind to find the answer, you will come to important realisations. For example, you can say to yourself, 'by reflecting on how you felt before you acknowledged your *whys* and how you felt after it, which *why* or set of *whys* had the most impact on you?' This process, when constantly carried out, becomes an amazing embellishing journey and experience in the world of the hearts and minds that will make us deeply relish life.

Stage 2: Practical planning

Once stage 1 is complete, you will feel motivated for wanting to express regular gratitude. Now, you must make a 'practical plan'. As they say 'if you fail to plan, you plan to fail.' Preparation and planning brings your chances of success to a high level. Depending on how well you have prepared, the chances of success will near 100%.

An example of your planning can be making a note in your calendar/diary/sticky note or on whatever you feel comfortable with, of a 1 month plan for expressing your gratitude. You can apply the following simple format:

Length of plan: what, when, how long for? How often?

Whys

Here is an example:

1 month + Gratitude Plan: express gratitude after breakfast for 10 minutes everyday.

Why?

1. You'll feel tranquillity, peace, serenity, joy, satisfaction, fulfillment, contentment and happiness.

2. You'll be able to grind it out easily to help you achieve your goals quickly with ease.

3. The negative feelings of stress, worry, anxiety, depression etc., will fade away.

The + sign above means the plan is for 1 month and will hopefully continue on after a month if there's no other reason not to. We make a 1 month plan so that we find it mentally easy to handle. It makes us feel motivated to implement it consistently since we have a target now. And targets serve to push us towards attaining them.

To give you more information on inputting the above plan, if you start the plan from today then you would note the above information within the note section of today's date on your calendar. You can use a diary or whatever you feel comfortable with. A month later from today you can note down something similar to '1 month gratitude plan over-evaluate/review.' This note would serve as a reminder to evaluate/review how the development went. You can ask yourself questions such as 'how did you feel before and after its implementation? How did it positively impact your life? How much more did you progress towards your goal the month after implementing it compared to the month before it?' These questions will help you to practically measure the return of success using 'the weight of progression' as a measurement once you finish your 1 month plan.

Just to reiterate, because you have a plan, it doesn't mean you can't upgrade it to a better version within the 1 month let's say, if an idea comes forth. Furthermore, you can tweak the template above and note it down for other gratitude habits you would like to inculcate within you such as buying gifts of appreciation, showing loving behaviour etc. This is the sort of format I have been using throughout my life and it has proven to be highly effective.

Stage 3: Implementation & process of self development

Practical planning will lead you to subconsciously knowing exactly what to do and in which situations. Even if you're not completely aware of the situation, you would react in the relevant situations with the planned manner but almost instinctively. Why? It is because you've re-programmed an aspect of your subconscious mind. Going through this somewhat instinctive reaction consistently, eventually seeing the characteristic become established within you, is an amazing journey that one must experience.

Let's focus now on the time just before the actual implementation. What I'm about to explain is more relevant to 'reactions in response to someone' than 'reactions that is not in response to someone.' An example of this can be the reaction of expressing appreciation to someone in response to them helping you.

When the time comes to implement an expression of gratitude, try your best to apply it. Subconsciously, you know what to do since you've planned it, which means you'll be confident. If you're still not confident, then you need to work on this weakness by constantly reminding yourself *why* you should have belief in yourself and be confident. If you fail, after exerting your utmost effort, accept it and move on. Don't feel down due to failing like this since you are actually in the process of development. Sometimes, it can take a few attempts before you can react with a new behaviour *properly*. It is like throwing a toddler into a pool to train them on how to swim. The initial few attempts will be failures. In other words, they'll be motioning their hands, arms, legs and feet incorrectly or in random directions. Nevertheless, it is still progression because by going through those failures they understand and feel their surroundings, in turn, keep getting better with more practice. And eventually, a beautiful scene captures our sight-the toddler is swimming! As they say, 'practice makes perfect.' What I have explained to you in this paragraph is the process of self development. You can use this knowledge and apply it with any new quality you want to embed within yourself as part of your self-development.

I will now highlight how one goes from their initial failure to enacting the quality in its proper form: after failing, the next time a similar situation arises, try again. Like before, you may complete the action but not properly. Nevertheless, the outcome would hopefully be better or closer to the proper form than your previous attempt. Keep trying no matter how many times you fail. Each time you try your best, despite failing, you are actually going through a process where you're *developing the ability* with which to complete this action properly. Eventually, your body transforms to a state where it is capable to accomplish that task in its proper form. This process that our body and mind undergoes happens when we try to inculcate within us a new behaviour or practice a new action properly. Here is another real life example to make you understand the process better: a person goes to the gym for the first time and has never used weights before. The first few attempts of lifting weights will usually be a bit shaky and not done in the proper form. He has failed to do it in the proper form despite exerting his utmost efforts. Now that his body has tasted some experience by actually feeling how it feels to lift those weights, he has a better idea of what to expect and is in a better position to succeed in lifting the weights with the proper form. Bear in mind, he knows very well how to do it as he has learnt about it, whether it was by watching a video or reading instructions. He just hasn't had practical experience. So he'll continue lifting. After several attempts, he gets better in his form. His body is transforming so that he can reach an upgraded state where he can lift weights properly. After three to five attempts where he fails but gets back up to try again, he lifts the weight properly with the correct form.

What one should do after the behaviour has developed is what I will now explain. Once the behaviour has developed to its proper level, it will become easier to implement. However, your due diligence of effort must still be exerted in order to keep the behaviour intact and developing to higher levels. From time to time, you may lose heed of behaving in the new, better way and experience the consequences of not observing this higher standard of behaviour. An example of such a consequence is not expressing thanks to someone using the correct tone and words in a situation where you were supposed to. To make the matter more clear, such consequence can be your partner not being as loving, caring and helpful as they normally are after you did not express gratitude/appreciation to them in the appropriate form in the situation you were supposed to. Someone in that situation, who is sincere in improving himself will reflect on why they have suffered those consequences. In other words, why their partner is not being as loving, caring and helpful as they normally are. They'll be looking for the *cause* of it. Eventually, they'll come to realise they have been through this situation before and will recall the solution (or reaction) they applied to overcome it, thus apply it, in turn, keep the harms at bay and enjoy the fruits of their correct behaviour.

"If you want to live like a king, fathom your basic blessings."

CHAPTER 7
Obstacles of Enacting Gratitude

7.1 Laziness

You don't feel like putting in the effort to exercise your brain to *think* in order to be grateful. You would feel discomfort in doing so. 'Maybe I can skip it for today' is what crosses your mind. Procrastination starts to creep in. And if it gets the better of you, it is going to be hard to implement the routine. You can be mentally defeated. Or you may feel you're weak and can't do it, in turn, cannot implement the gratitude routine. Here is a strong solution for such a situation: you remind yourself of *why* you need to overcome discomfort and laziness in order to have gratitude. As I said before, the *whys* are deeply powerful. Having said that, if we hasten the process of acknowledging our *whys* without enacting it properly, it would prove to be ineffective. Here are some impelling *whys*:

- One reason that really motivates me is my passion to be a champion. I tell myself that if people out there who have been successful, can be disciplined - i.e., when they don't feel like doing what they're supposed to, they'll still do it - then so can you. Rather, you can do even better because you know you can work harder and smarter than them. Then I would remind myself of all the competitions and successes I have achieved in my life. By the end of it, I would feel charged up with positivity and empowered, thereby continue being consistent in expressing gratitude or continue to focus on developing a character trait I'm working on with quality. It would be quality as the motivation I have gained will lead me to being diligently focused. Subsequently, I would succeed in conquering laziness.

⬥ Another reason that is a strong motivating factor for me to continue on, despite not feeling to do so, finding it boring or discomforting, is realising how if I don't continue to remain focused, the chances of achieving my lofty aspirations will reduce. And one slack can cost dearly. From it, I can lose 6 months worth of progression or even more. The way to fathom this reality is to realise that the road to progression brings with it exponential growth. This is a known law of the universe. As a matter of fact, the universe itself is exponentially growing as we speak. Furthermore, exponential growth is a reality that we experience in our lives. For example, regarding my entrepreneurial journey, when I compare how fast I progressed initially to the later stages, I noticed a big difference. That initially the progression was slow. A lot of patience was required to keep going. It took time to understand simple concepts in business whereas now I can learn multiple times more new concepts and understand it quicker. Initially, it took time to implement a component of the business because I had no prior experience before doing so. In contrast, later on, I could complete actions pertaining to a lot more components in a short span of time. Over time, through the experience and knowledge we gain, we become more efficient in running processes or enacting successful business models. In other words, we progress multiple times faster towards our goal later on, when working towards it, compared to the beginning stages, so long as we're continuing to exert the utmost of our ability like we did during the beginning stages. In business, they call this phenomenon, 'the snowball effect' which means that as the snowball is rolled, the snow becomes multiple times larger over time. Therefore, slacking makes you lose out on a measure of exponential growth that you had the potential to attain during that period of time you slacked. Since progression is exponential, in the long term, if you compare the state of achievement you would reach without slacking compared to the state of achievement you would reach with slacking, there would be an enormous gap. This can amount to 6 months or even years. So one must acknowledge this reality and be willing to do whatever work they need to do whether they feel like doing it or not so that they can achieve their dreams very quickly, leaving legacies before they know it.

By choosing to be lazy which includes procrastination or doing that which has a lower priority, we would make it hard for ourselves to return back to our best. Consequently, a measure of exponential progression would be lost despite returning back to our best. Realising this is another reason for overcoming laziness. I will elaborate on this aspect to make the matter more clear: as I said, if we constantly choose to be lazy by not doing what we're supposed to or prioritising the insignificant tasks over the significant ones, eventually when we want to start progressing again, it would be very hard compared to before. Why is that? Because our soul has become accustomed to being lazy or not wanting to do that which is *significant*. So we would have to strive really hard to return back to our best state where we're consistently choosing to do the most significant tasks. In other words, if we decided from the get-go to choose the option of *not* overcoming our laziness and doing the *insignificant* task, then the effort of hard work that we have to put in to return back to our best would be more than choosing initially to do the *significant* task. Looking at it from a different perspective, if we compare the two states, we would come to realise the gap in the difference of benefits and amount of progression. That the initial option of overcoming our laziness to complete the *significant* task would require *less effort* but bear more fruits in terms of achievement compared to the option of choosing to be lazy by doing the *insignificant* task. This leads to a slippery slope, thus finding it harder to overcome our laziness. It also leads to a loss of potential progression and eventually when we do complete the task we are supposed to, after choosing to be lazy for some time, the effort required to return back to our best is a lot more. Therefore, potential progression, exponential in size, has been lost.

You may be wondering what I mean when I say *significant* task. What I mean is focusing on the bigger picture or applying the 20/80 principle. The 20/80 principle is an extremely powerful mindset. Entrepreneurs love it and therefore always employ it. It is focusing on the 20% that produces 80% of the result. The 20% are the main components/foundation of achieving something. For example, in business, the 20% components could be: product/service, price and marketing.

If the best product is picked, the best pricing is given and the best marketing – the 20% - is employed, then there can be a good level of sales/profits, which is the 80%. The enaction of this principle makes things very efficient, leading you to live your dreams faster than you'd expect.

7.2 Not realising the value of gratitude:

Sometimes we may lose farsightedness and only see what is immediate. As a result, we may be conscious of how exercising gratitude can make us feel good but see the benefits of enacting gratitude limited to that – feeling good. This usually happens after some time when we stop reminding ourselves of the long term and deep benefits of gratitude and how it is an investment to exponential progression and success. Seeing the value of gratitude in a limited fashion can also take place when we're constantly busy doing things and not taking out some time to reflect. In these situations, we may see gratitude as simply a virtue or something confined to spirituality which has nothing to do with achieving our aspirations. This can make us negligent of regularly expressing gratitude, in turn, head back to the path of dullness, misery, being unhappy, finding life difficult, hating life etc. So the question is 'how can we overcome this?' In these situations where we perceive gratitude in limited ways, we should take out some time to ask ourselves some questions so that we realise the great value of gratitude. Here are some questions we can ask ourselves:

1. Why should I take out some time every day to be grateful?

2. How can gratitude lead me to achieving my goals/dreams quickly?

3. How much of a progression have I made in the past, after exercising gratitude regularly compared to recently when it hasn't been so regular?

After completing this exercise, we would see the great importance of prioritising a short amount of time to express gratitude daily or enact different forms of gratitude whenever appropriate. Thereby, in the long run, heedlessness that can make us lose sight of the profound value of exercising gratitude will diminish. This ensures exponential progression is at its optimum, in turn, achieving our dreams quickly without losing quality whilst being truly happy.

"Gratitude is a profitable investment that will always give you returns."

CHAPTER 8
Earnest Effective Gratitude

8.1 Sincerity in recalling relevant blessings:

This life is imperfect. And so our journey to being grateful will also have imperfections. Sometimes, recalling our favours during our daily 10-15 minutes of expressing gratitude may not be as effective as we ought it to be. And that is because we are focusing on *general* things to be grateful for or that bounty which we are remembering is not relevant to our current state. Although remembering these types of blessings will bring good feelings, it will not necessarily provide us that deeper feeling of tranquillity, contentment, satisfaction, happiness and appreciation that we should feel. Like with anything, gratitude has its levels. So in order to reach a higher level of gratitude we should remember those gifts that are relevant to our state. And a key factor in achieving this is being sincere and honest with ourselves. We sincerely ask ourselves during this time, 'why should you be grateful?' And then we genuinely think for an answer. By doing so, we will find those successes and gifts we have, in turn, feel deep joy, happiness, fulfillment and contentment. This is contrary to just robotically recalling the same blessings or many general blessings routinely without being genuine in the process, feeling it or making our heart and mind present during it. By not being focused with the presence of our heart and mind, the effect of gratitude will be very low. Take myself for example, I have experienced that sometimes, the type of gratitude I need to observe is one that goes deep. I may have to recall that low point in my life, realising that no one could help me. So ultimately I can't rely on anyone. I have to rely on my Helper who has given me the tools of mind and heart, through which I was guided to researching, discovering and learning vital lessons in relation to my extremely low state. It was an awakening for me. After application of pertinent knowledge that resulted from this awakening, I rose up from the depths of the dark ocean, feeling like a completely new person, ree from the shackles of slavery - a great portion of it being slavery to the opinions of people.

3.2 Recalling specific blessings

Sometimes, during the middle of the day, we don't feel good. We don't feel like doing work. We find it hard to continue taking action to progress towards our goal because we don't want to feel the discomfort and pain of doing so. If we are of those who regularly practice gratitude by reminding ourselves during times like this, of the great success we have already achieved so that we feel better and rejuvenated to continue on, then on this occasion, that reminder of our great success proves to not be so effective. It is not effective in the sense that by recalling the usual/general blessings we have, it doesn't give us that good feeling which propels us to continue on like it usually does. So what I've discovered is that for various situations there are specific types of blessings or acknowledgements we need to make in order to effectively feel grateful and content with what we have. This of course makes it easy for us to continue doing the work necessary to achieve our goals. The specific blessings one must recall can differ from person to person. You would come to know or realise with experience, which type of acknowledgement(s) or recalling of blessing(s) would make you feel rejuvenated. You would acknowledge these specific blessings to the level where you now find it easy to continue on doing the work required to progress towards your goal. For example: it's midday. I don't feel like completing the work necessary to progress towards my goal. I just don't feel good. So I enact gratitude by reflecting and realising how successful I already am with my accomplishments. I still don't feel like continuing on. It has proved to not to be so effective. So I would now recall a different blessing. I would reflect and realise how I'm in a state of peace and don't have stress. In the past, I've been in situations where I felt stressed due to problems that I was challenged with. All I wanted was peace during that state. Right now, I have peace and no stress. So i've got nothing to complain about. Therefore, I'll just accept the minor discomfort of continuing to do works of progression towards my goal. The discomfort and pain is nothing compared to the other situations I've been in.

Throughout the exercise of recalling the worst of situations I've been in, I do so trying to feel as accurately as possible how I felt during that scenario in the past, thus comparing those negative feelings of pain and discomfort to the ones I'm currently feeling. Now I would feel really grateful realising how insignificant my current pains and discomforts are.

Moreover, I feel rejuvenated and motivated to continue on. Recalling this specific blessing has proved to be more effective in this situation than recalling my general successes and accomplishments.

CHAPTER 9

The Amazing Power of Noting Down Expressions of Gratitude

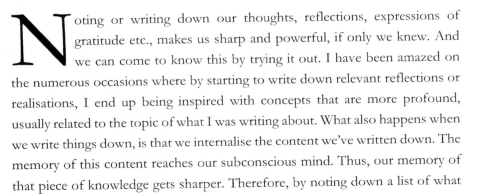

Noting or writing down our thoughts, reflections, expressions of gratitude etc., makes us sharp and powerful, if only we knew. And we can come to know this by trying it out. I have been amazed on the numerous occasions where by starting to write down relevant reflections or realisations, I end up being inspired with concepts that are more profound, usually related to the topic of what I was writing about. What also happens when we write things down, is that we internalise the content we've written down. The memory of this content reaches our subconscious mind. Thus, our memory of that piece of knowledge gets sharper. Therefore, by noting down a list of what we should be grateful for or content with, our *quality* of gratitude will be higher.

When it comes to using this technique to help me be grateful and content, usually what I would do is write down a list of the worst case scenarios that can happen during the current stage of my life. By being content with the worst case scenarios, we feel a deep inner cool breeze of gratitude and contentment. This contentment of the worst case scenario mindset helps us to overcome the fear of failure, as it generates the mindset 'I have nothing to lose and everything to gain.' In other words, I don't fear failing after realising that despite the worst case scenario occurring, it won't be as bad as that extremely low point of my existence where I felt I couldn't continue on with life. Therefore, whatever worst case scenario that occurs, it won't be as bad as that point. So long as I'm trying to do the right and best thing, that's all that matters. So I'll just continue to enjoy living my life. In other words, enjoy the process of completing actions in trying to make my dreams a reality and this enjoyment is not halted due to failure occuring. Furthermore, I realise I'm still very successful. That despite the failure, I still have succeeded because I am in a better position to succeed on the next attempt since I've gained more experience by trying it out. Therefore, anything else I gain is a bonus, hence the terms 'everything to gain.' So I will relax, take it easy, try my best and enjoy the process of trying my best to achieve something regardless of the outcome. So long as I exerted my utmost means after learning and knowing how to do it properly, that's all that matters. Writing the relevant information pertaining to this made me deeply internalise it, in turn, feel immense gratefulness and contentment enter inside me, like a swift breezy wind.

Notes on the worst case scenarios or realisations need to be made when the fear of '*what if*' appears as thoughts in our hearts and minds. 'What if I don't succeed with this business? What if I lose my job? What if my partner leaves me?' etc. The thought beginning with *what if* can be dangerous if we don't know how to deal with it. The fear can lead to mental, in turn, physical illnesses and can even lead to us taking out our own lives if it gets really bad. So the way I would deal with it is by thinking of the worst case scenario and being content with it. I would literally write the title resembling something similar to the following: 'Worst case-contentment:' Then, I would write down what's the worst that could happen and in reality what is likely to happen. Here is an example:

If I end up not succeeding with this business, then I'm still thankful, happy and content. That is because at least I've learnt and developed in terms of implementing this component of business, thus have a better chance next time. I still have extra money, food, clothes shelter, family, a good life etc.

Reality: You are likely to succeed since most people who have applied strategies you are looking to apply, have succeeded. Furthermore, you have succeeded in other components of the business up to this stage so be confident you will succeed.

Returning back to our key point in this section of 'noting down our expressions of gratitude,' this can be done in various ways. Some choose to include notes of gratitude in a diary. Others may opt to note things down on their phones. Whatever the case, if we have a plan to acquire the objective of 'noting down our expressions of gratitude', when we need to, we will succeed. I just want to emphasise and highlight the *why* of noting down expressions of gratitude as it is core in importance: we are noting down expressions of gratitude when we feel we are lacking in gratitude (usually when we're always focusing on our wants) because we want to have deep gratitude and contentment so that we can feel tranquillity, serenity, satisfaction, fulfillment, peace, happiness, success, appreciation, joy and more. Acknowledging this will lead us to being rejuvenated to continue on in achieving our goals. Furthermore, noting down our expressions of gratitude will result in achieving more in a span of time compared to not doing so. Thus, our goal will be achieved faster whilst keeping to quality standards in the process towards it.

CHAPTER 10
Examples of Worst Case Scenarios for Deep Gratitude and Contentment

In this section, I will give examples of common scenarios we can face and what the worst case scenarios may be, to demonstrate the process that directs us to truly feeling an abundance of tranquillity, contentment, serenity, peace etc., poured into our hearts. When we honestly accept in our hearts the worst case scenario, that if it were to take place, I'm still content/happy because I still have such and such - only then will such acceptance make us experience pleasant deep feelings abundantly entering into our hearts. Below are several examples pertaining to this reality followed by other important related points.

10.1 Scenario 1: I may lose my job as the company decides to make redundant some employees.

Thinking towards gratefulness: "If I lose my job, then I'm still content and grateful that I have gained experience which can help me to easily get another job. I am fortunate to have had a job and earnt some money since many cannot find jobs easily due to the competitiveness for vacancies. Also, up to this point, I have enjoyed living a good life. I've had healthy food to eat, good clothes to wear, a roof over my head, a laptop, a phone, a car etc. I still have savings. So at least for now, I can continue to enjoy living life. There are people out there who are living on the streets. If I was in their situation I would feel miserable, weak, cold, low and dream of getting a comfortable night's sleep. I feel so at peace that I actually don't have to experience that state and I actually have what they are dreaming of. Furthermore, there are those in other parts of the world who are walking many miles, exerting hardwork, putting in a lot of effort and sweating, just to carry a limited amount of water into their container, brought from the well. In contrast, all I have to do is just switch on the tap and after a few seconds have been supplied with multiple times more water than them. I have had the privilege to use my free time to learn, develop and experience so many wonderful things of life that they haven't. Wow! What a good life I've been granted!"

By now, I would genuinely feel my heart being filled with chunks of natural rich tranquil and serene feelings. At this stage, life is very relaxing, enjoyable and stress free. However, there is a trap here that could prove counterproductive. We may now start to feel content so much so that we feel we don't need to strive hard to achieve our goals. We don't feel like doing anything. We just want to relax and not do anything productive. If we don't take care of this feeling and attitude, it can lead us to feeling lazy, lethargic, sleeping a lot, feeling weak, slow and unsuccessful. So in order to ensure we don't head towards that direction, we should realise:

I'm content but I still have to continue striving my utmost to continue working on my online business project (or any other goal) as I still *need and want* to attain financial independence (or whatever objective it is that you want to achieve). I still want to be a champion. I still want to do great good works for humanity at large. I still want to provide a better life for my family. I still want to leave a legacy and add positively to civilisation. I still want to achieve my utmost potential in this life. And the list goes on.

10.2 Scenario 2: My partner may leave me

Thinking towards gratefulness: "If I lose him/her, then I'm still content and grateful as I've learnt a lot from this relationship. I'm grateful to have been given an opportunity to be in a relationship in the first place. There are those who don't find partners at all during their lives. How sad must their state be. At least I've had the privilege of experiencing a relationship. I can learn from this relationship, research further to find out any other causes of failure for this relationship. Thereafter, I will be stronger for my next relationship. In other words, have a better chance of success. So it's not the end of the world. At least for now I can take a break and achieve any goals that I wanted to achieve without any stress or distractions that I used to face whilst with my partner.

Furthermore, it's not like I don't have the basic necessities of life that my life is so hard right now. I'm grateful that I still have good food to eat, nice clothes to wear, a home where I can sleep comfortably in, family and friends with whom I can enjoy socialising with. I can still give and attain love to some extent from them. At least, I'm not in a country where there is a war going on. Where they can't live in peace but are always in a state of worry and suffer severe pains from the harms that result from the war. I'm so fortunate to not be in such a country. Considering everything I have, I'm actually living a high quality life people would dream of but never get. I feel such a high level of peace now. Losing my partner is nothing considering all the other great blessings I still have."

Thinking in this manner, like with the previous scenario, will cause immense tranquil and serene feelings to enter within your heart. If you had actually lost your partner in some way and you've exercised the relevant thinking process towards gratefulness and felt the tranquil, serene feelings it has brought, realise as always, there is a trap. This trap is thinking you will not be bothered again by the thought of losing the woman you loved. Be aware that nothing in this life is perfect. Therefore, this thinking towards gratefulness alone will not make you reach the state where you won't be bothered at all in the future at the thought of realising your partner has left you. So like with anything else, from time to time, when you feel the need, you'll need to remind yourself of why you should still be grateful despite losing her. What I mean by 'feel the need' is feeling low or negative feelings due to remembering thoughts pertaining to the loss of your spouse.

In the long run, it will become easier to overcome any feelings of pain, negativity and lowness that can naturally arrive at your heart from these thoughts. This is because the *whys* of continuing to be content, despite the loss, is entrenched into your heart and mind. It has become entrenched after you've consistently reminded yourself of these *whys* when struck with the realisation that the one whom you loved is no longer with you. It could be any thoughts in relation to her that brings you down, especially good memories.

10.3 Scenario 3: I got into a car accident and have lost an arm

Thinking towards gratefulness: "I've lost my arm but I should still be content and grateful. Why? It could be worse. Imagine I lost my life. Then I would not be able to achieve my goals at all! At least without an arm I still have the potential to achieve my goals, since I can use the other arm. There are people out there who don't have any arms or legs. Imagine I was in their situation. I would feel weak, dependent and cannot achieve what I want to achieve in life. In addition, I cannot enjoy taking a stroll, I cannot enjoy having food with my own hands nor brush my own teeth. But the reality is, I can do all these things which they can't. People would pay anything to have a pair of hands and feet like myself. Furthermore, I still have money, food, clothes, water, a home where I feel at peace and can get a good night's rest. At least I managed to get a good education, have friends and family who will look out for me. I've been blessed with so many blessings! How fortunate am I?! I have no reason to complain!"

10.4 Scenario 4: I lose my life in trying to stand up for justice/what is right

Thinking towards gratefulness: "I've tried my best to be truthful and honest in all that I do. I'd rather leave this world honourably by standing up for the truth/justice which results in my departure from life rather than compromise and end up still being attacked/harmed due to not standing up for it. And thereby, achieve a weak, disgraceful demise. If I don't stand up for my rights, I can be taken advantage of and oppressed. If that were to happen, I would feel weak, degraded, disgraced and possibly harmed physically. Therefore, I would rather fight for my rights and hopefully attain it as well as the honour and praise of people that comes along with it. How many people have fought for their rights and succeeded? And how many people left a legacy, remembered in history because they stood up for justice?"

After thinking like this, I should be in a state where I feel inspired, motivated and empowered, being content with the worst case scenario of losing my life in the face of standing up for my rights. I can now continue on, willing to face any challenge and stand up for what is right.

10.5 Internalisation through noting

From time to time, when I am at my lowest, I would make brief notes on my phone calendar titled 'Contentment-Worst case scenarios'. These worst case scenarios would be connected to the fear, worry and stress I would be feeling during that time. By noting things down, our thoughts become organised and clear. This leads to the points becoming internalised better, thus acquiring of high quality contentment and gratefulness is achieved. After this, we'd feel rejuvenated to continue taking action towards achieving our goals.

10.6 Shifting focus from negative to positive

You may come to realise after reading the above scenarios that as soon as something negative affects us, we naturally tend to focus on that negative aspect. As a result, it makes dark the treasures and valuables money can't buy, that we have. Hence why we must train ourselves to shift our focus from that which is negative to the many positives we already have. The reality is, we hold vast amounts of treasures, blessings and goodness compared to the negatives. The ratio of blessings we have to the negatives may be around 10:1. However, some of us are ignorant of this reality and as a result, suffer the consequences of magnifying the negative. Therefore, we must always realise that we have far more positives than negatives.

CHAPTER 11

Obstacle of Enaction - 'I don't have time'

S ome people struggle to make time for self-development, perceiving it to be a task holding little significance. They need to realise that time is always available. It is down to us to prioritise what we give time for and be efficient in using up our time by which 'we will have time' for the important things. It's because we don't see the long term exponential benefits and progression that can come out from *investing* time into personal development as entrepreneurs and billionaires do. We are short sighted at times. Even then, if someone still finds it difficult to make time for expressing gratitude, I challenge them to spend at least five minutes every day. Five minutes out of the 1440 minutes we have in a day. We spend a lot of time on social media, doing something that is not so important or wasting time. I'm sure we can at least cut down five minutes from that time for something that can immensely change our lives for the better.

Realise that if you do spend five minutes everyday reading this book and enjoy doing so, i'm sure you would eventually spend a lot more than five minutes. Why? Because it is something you enjoy doing. And what we enjoy doing, we value, hence would make time for it.

I hope by now you have acknowledged the grandeur of this noble characteristic-gratitude. It is a broad, vast characteristic that is the mother of benefits and dispeller of harms. It is a quality that rescues you in your darkest and lowest of times. And it does so even when you're on the brink of suicide. Deep, rich long lasting tranquillity, serenity, peace and happiness are the outcome of manifesting this characteristic in our lives. Hence why we must prioritise and invest time into inculcating this value within us. One who does so will not regret embarking on this journey but rather be grateful for being led to this change in his life.

Finally, I hope you have exercised and developed gratitude during the course of reading this book. I also hope you have experienced wonders, immense benefits, tranquillity, happiness, bliss, peace, fulfillment, satisfaction, serenity, appreciation, joy and contentment whilst on this amazing empowering journey.

Acknowledgements

I thank my mother for always being supportive, showing immense love, care, always being there for me and bringing me up in the best way. I thank my father for having confidence in me, providing for me during my early years, looking out for me and being supportive. I thank my brother for being very supportive, thinking highly of me, encouraging and motivating me and being a good friend. I thank my sister for her support, encouragement, respect and generosity. I thank my relatives who have always been very supportive and hospitable. I thank the Arqam team especially Sheikh for the knowledge, opportunity, inspiration, motivation, advice, support and encouragement that lead to a good portion of my development. I thank my close friends without whom I would not be the great person I am today. They have always been very supportive, caring and helped me in different walks of life when faced with challenges. I thank all those who have had a positive impact in my life. I thank Kindle Direct Publishing for providing me with this platform of opportunity to publish this book. Ultimately, I thank my Lord, without whom I could not have achieved this endeavour. The One who assisted me in my most challenging and difficult of times when nobody else could.

About the Author

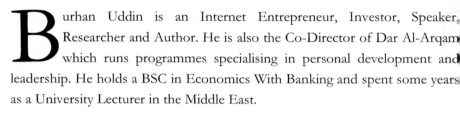

Burhan Uddin is an Internet Entrepreneur, Investor, Speaker, Researcher and Author. He is also the Co-Director of Dar Al-Arqam which runs programmes specialising in personal development and leadership. He holds a BSC in Economics With Banking and spent some years as a University Lecturer in the Middle East.

Due to the challenges he has faced early in his life, he has gained valuable lessons, performed extensive research and studies on important principles pertaining to self-help and self-development. His mission is to help others also overcome challenges, difficulties and sufferings they are facing in life as well as to achieve their goals/dreams quickly and easily. He will use his decade of research, knowledge and experience to help them in their endeavour.

What Did You Think of Gratitude to Greatness: Proven Practices Producing Profound Success?

First of all, thank you for purchasing this book Gratitude to Greatness: Proven Practices Producing Profound Success. I know you could have picked any number of books to read, but you picked this book and for that I am extremely grateful.

I hope that it added value and quality to your everyday life. If so, it would be really nice if you could share this book with your friends and family by posting to Facebook *and* Twitter.

Printed in Great Britain
by Amazon

40491271R00037